CW00689888

LINCOLN TO CLEETHORPES

Vic Mitchell and Keith Smith

MP Middleton Press

Front cover: Gates and signals from the past adorn Stallingborough. No. 156423 forms the 09.00 from Newark North Gate to Cleethorpes on 17th March 1992. (M.J.Stretton)

Back cover upper: The complex ownership of the routes in Lincoln is shown on the Railway Clearing House diagram of 1908.

Back cover lower: Near Cleethorpes Lakeside on 9th July 2001 is Bassett Lowke 4-4-2 no. 1 Sutton Belle. *It was built in 1933. (P.G.Barnes)*

Published March 2014

ISBN 978 1 908174 56 7

© Middleton Press, 2014

Design Deborah Esher
Typesetting Barbara Mitchell

Published by
>   *Middleton Press*
>   *Easebourne Lane*
>   *Midhurst*
>   *West Sussex*
>   *GU29 9AZ*
Tel: 01730 813169
Fax: 01730 812601
Email: info@middletonpress.co.uk
www.middletonpress.co.uk

Printed in the United Kingdom by Henry Ling Limited, at the Dorset Press, Dorchester, DT1 1HD

INDEX

ACKNOWLEDGEMENTS

We are very grateful for the assistance received from many of those mentioned in the credits, also to R.S.Carpenter, A.J.Castledine, G.Croughton, G.Gartside, D.A.Johnston, N.Langridge, B.Lewis, M.J.Lloyd, J.P.McCrickard, Mr D. and Dr S.Salter, T.Walsh, E.Wilmshurst and in particular, our always supportive wives, Barbara Mitchell and Janet Smith.

I. British Railways route map for 1964.

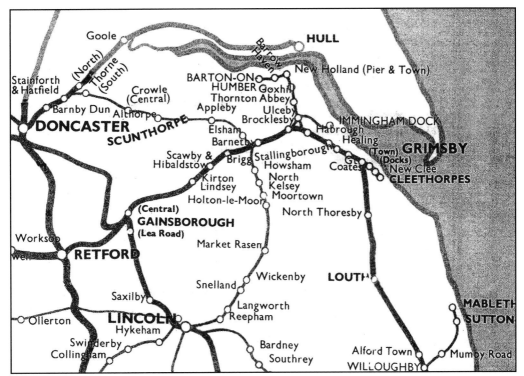

GEOGRAPHICAL SETTING

The historic city of Lincoln is noted for its massive cathedral and its commercial importance as the county town. It is situated on the east flowing River Witham, which enters the North Sea near Boston. It has cut a gap in the limestone ridge, which runs across England from Dorset to the River Humber and is known as The Cotswolds in its middle section. The gap in Lincoln Heath attracted seven railway routes to aim for Lincoln.

Our line runs north as far as Barnetby on nearly flat land, but here it turns almost east to pass over a low ridge of chalk, which forms the northern extension of the Lincolnshire Wolds. This deposit has been of commercial value, but the chalk over which the remainder of the route passes was not so.

Grimsby is situated at the mouth of the Humber and has been noted for its fish traffic for centuries. Scandinavian timber has been another notable import, while coal was for long an important export. South of the town, Cleethorpes grew as a popular leisure resort, following the arrival of the railway.

The maps are to the scale of 25ins to 1 mile, with north at the top, unless otherwise indicated.

Gradient profile for the northern part of the route. The southern section is mostly level.

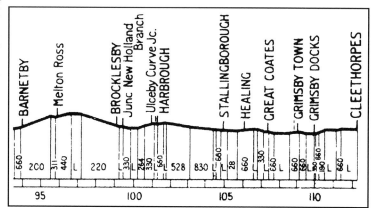

HISTORICAL BACKGROUND

The line from Lincoln to Grimsby was built under an Act of July 1846 and was opened on 18th December 1848, between Lincoln and Market Rasen. The section north to Usselby had come into use on 1st November 1848, but the route to Grimsby had been opened first, on 1st March 1848 by the Manchester, Sheffield & Lincolnshire Railway. This included a branch to New Holland.

Lincoln had been reached by the Midland Railway from Nottingham in 1846. The Great Northern Railway arrived in Lincoln from Boston in 1848 and ran north to Gainsborough in 1849. The route west to Tuxford came into use in 1896 and became part of the Great Central Railway. The MS&LR became the main part of the GCR, when it was formed in 1897. Lincoln was served by the GNR from Grantham from 1867 and Sleaford from 1882.

Further north, Barnetby had MS&LR trains from Gainsborough from 1849 and from Scunthorpe from 1882, although the route was opened in 1866 by the Trent, Ancholme & Grimsby Railway.

The first company to reach Grimsby was the East Lincolnshire Railway, which ran north from Boston from 1848. The MS&LR extended its network from Grimsby to Cleethorpes on 6th April 1863. The Grimsby to Immingham line was completed in 1906.

The MR became part of the London Midland & Scottish Railway in 1923 and the GCR and the GNR then became constituents of the London & North Eastern Railway. Upon nationalisation in 1948, most of the LMSR formed the London Midland Region of British Railways, while much of the LNER became its Eastern Region.

The route of this album was operated by Central Trains from 2nd March 1997, following privatisation. The franchisee became East Midland on 11th November 2007, most trains originating at Cleethorpes.

PASSENGER SERVICES

Only trains running the main length of the route will be considered in this volume. The down direction is used and only trains running five or more days per week are listed.

In many years, particularly recently, the Sunday service has been operated only in the Summer, especially on the Grimsby-Cleethorpes section. Destinations will be revealed in many of the captions.

	Weekdays	Sundays
1850	4	2
1865	6	3
1884	6	2
1905	6	2
1918	4	2
1925	5	0
1944	4	0
1965	7	0
1985	10	4
2005	7	3

CLEETHORPES, GREAT GRIMSBY, NEW HOLLAND, and HULL.—Manchester, Sheffield, and Lincolnshire.

(timetable — Week Days and Sundays)

November 1865

February 1884

HULL, MARKET RASEN, and LINCOLN.—Manchester, Sheffield, and Lincolnshire.

(timetable — Up and Down, Week Days and Sundays)

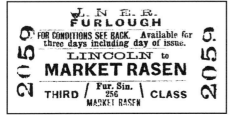

LINCOLN, MARKET RASEN, HULL, GRIMSBY, and CLEETHORPES.—Great Central.

Miles	Up.	Week Days. mrn (Calls at Riby St. at 8 28 mrn.)	aft	aft	aft	Sundays. mrn	Sundays. aft
	Lincoln (High St) dep.	6 30	1 25	3 44	8 30	5 40	2 50
4¾	Reepham ....[by	6 41	1 35	3 54	8 40	5 54	3 0
6½	Langworth, for Wrag-	6 45	1 39	3 58	8 44	5 58	3 4
9¼	Snelland	6 51	1 45	4 4	8 51	6 4	3 11
11	Wickenby	6 55	1 49	4 8	8 55	6 8	3 15
15	Market Rasen	7 4	1 58	4 18	9 4	6 17	3 24
17¾	Claxby and Usselby	7 10	2 4	4 24	9 10	6 23	3 30
20¼	Holton	7 15	2 9	4 29	Sig.	6 28	3 36
22	Moortown*	7 19	2 13	4 33	9 19	6 32	3 40
23½	North Kelsey	7 23	2 17	4 37	9 23	6 36	3 44
25½	Howsham	7 28	2 22	4 42	Sig.	6 41	3 49
28½	Barnetby 698 .. arr.	7 35	2 30	4 50	9 35	6 48	3 58
	Barnetby 698 .. dep.	7 39	2 31	4 52	9 36	6 50	3 59
34¼	Brocklesby ...... arr.	7 47	2 39	4 59	9 44	6 58	4 7
41¾	706 New Holland arr.	8 43	3 28	5 30	1015	7 58	5 18
44¾	706 Hull † ...... "	9 20	4 10	6 30	1050	8 45	5 50
—	Brocklesby ...... dep.	7 49	2 40	5 0	9 45	6 59	4 8
36	Habrough	7 54	2 44	5 4	9 49	7 3	4 12
39¾	Stallingboro'	8 3	2 53	5 12	k	7 11	4 20
40¾	Healing	8 6	2 56	5 15	k	7 14	4 23
42	Great Coates	8 9	2 59	5 18	k	7 17	4 27
44	Grimsby Town 406	8 14	3 4	5 23	10 3	7 22	4 32
45	Grimsby Docks	8 26	3 12	5 30	1010	7 40	4 40
45¾	New Clee	8 32	3 16	5 34	1014	7 44	4 44
47¼	Cleethorpes .... arr.	8 36	3 20	5 38	1018	7 48	4 48

Miles	Down.	Week Days. mrn	mrn	aft	Sundays. mrn	Sundays. aft
	Cleethorpes .... dep.	7 5	9 50	5 45	8 25	5 20
1¼	New Clee	7 10	9 55	5 50	8 30	5 26
2¼	Grimsby Docks	7 15	10 2	5 55	8 35	5 31
3¾	Grimsby Town 406	7 20	10 7	6 1	8 40	5 37
5¼	Great Coates	7 25	a	6 6	8 45	5 42
6½	Healing	7 28	a	6 9	8 48	5 45
7¾	Stallingboro'	7 31	a	6 12	8 51	5 48
11¼	Habrough	7 42	1023	6 21	9 0	5 57
13	Brocklesby ...... arr.	7 46	1027	6 25	9 4	6 1
—	706 Hull † ...... dep.	6 37	9 37	5 7	7 42	3 57
—	706 New Holland "	7 20	1015	6 0	8 15	4 30
—	Brocklesby ...... dep.	7 47	1028	6 26	9 5	6 2
17¾	Barnetby ...... arr.	7 55	1036	6 34	9 14	6 11
	Barnetby ...... dep.	7 59	1048	6 40	9 15	6 13
21¼	Howsham	8 7	1056	6 48	9 23	6 21
23¾	North Kelsey	8 11	11 0	6 52	9 27	6 25
25¼	Moortown*	8 15	11 4	6 56	9 31	6 29
26¾	Holton	8 20	11 8	7 0	9 35	6 33
29½	Claxby and Usselby	8 26	1115	7 7	9 42	6 40
32½	Market Rasen	8 33	1123	7 15	9 50	6 48
36¼	Wickenby	8 41	1131	7 23	9 58	6 56
37¾	Snelland ....[by	8 46	1136	7 28	10 3	7 1
41	Langworth, for Wrag-	8 52	1142	7 34	10 9	7 7
42¾	Reepham ..[359, 395	9 0	1150	7 38	1013	7 13
47¼	Lincoln ¶ 358, arr.	9 10	12 1	7 50	1025	7 25

a Takes up for Brocklesby and beyond on giving notice at the Station.

k Stops to set down from Barnetby or beyond on notice being given to the Guard at Barnetby.

* Station for Caistor (2¾ miles).

† Corporation Pier (by Boat).

¶ High Street Station.

July 1918

September 1925

LINCOLN, MARKET RASEN, HULL, GRIMSBY, and CLEETHORPES.—L. & N. E.

Miles	Up.	Week Days only. mrn	mrn	mrn	aft	aft (Fridays only.)	aft	aft
	Lincoln (L.N.E.) dep.	5 20		8 35	1 25	2 55	3 50	8 30
4¾	Reepham (Lincs.).[by	5 34		8 45	1 35	....	4 0	8 40
6½	Langworth, for Wrag-	5 38		8 49	1 39	3 7	4 4	8 44
9¼	Snelland	5 44		8 55	1 45	3 13	4 10	8 50
11	Wickenby	5 48		8 59	1 49	....	4 14	8 54
15	Market Rasen	5 57		9 8	1 58	3 23	4 23	9 4
17¾	Claxby and Usselby	6 3		9 14	2 4	....	4 29	9 10
20¼	Holton-le-Moor	6 8		9 20	2 9	....	4 35	Dd
22	Moortown A	6 13		9 24	2 13	3 33	4 39	9 19
23½	North Kelsey	6 17		9 29	2 17	3 37	4 43	9 23
25½	Howsham	6 22		9 34	2 22	....	4 48	Dd
29½	Barnetby 814.. arr.	6 29		9 41	2 30	3 45	4 55	9 35
	Barnetby 814.. dep.	6 33	9 44	9 51	2 36	4 2	4 56	9 36
34¼	Brocklesby ...... arr.	6 40	....	9 58	2 43	4 10	5F3	9 43
41¾	821 New Holland arr.	7 12	....	1055	3 21	....	5 40	1014
44¾	821 Hull B ...... "	7 40	....	1125	4 5	....	6 20	1050
—	Brocklesby ...... dep.	6 42	....	....	2 44	4 12	5F4	9 44
36	Habrough	6 47	9 55	....	2 49	4 16	5 7	9 49
39¾	Stallingboro'	6 56	10 3	....	2 58	4 24	5 14	Kk
40¾	Healing	6 59	10 6	....	3 1	4 27	5 17	9 57
42	Great Coates	7 2	1010	....	3 4	....	5 21	Kk
44	Grimsby Town 735	7 7	1015	....	3 9	4 34	5 25	10 3
45	Grimsby Docks	7 19	1025	....	3 17	4 44	5 32	1010
45¾	New Clee	7 25	1029	....	3 21	4 48	5 36	....
47¼	Cleethorpes .... arr.	7 29	1033	....	3 25	4 52	5 40	1016

Miles	Down.	Week Days only. mrn	mrn	mrn (Fridays only.)	aft	aft	aft
	Cleethorpes .... dep.	7 5	9 43	1040	3 5	5 25	....
1¼	New Clee	7 10	9 48	1045	3 10	5 30	....
2¼	Grimsby Docks	7 15	9 53	1053	3 19	5 35	....
3¾	Grimsby Town 735	7 20	10 5	11 5	3 26	5 42	....
5¼	Great Coates	7 25	1010	Aa	3 31	5 47	....
6½	Healing	7 28	Aa	1112	3 35	5 50	....
7¾	Stallingboro'	7 31	Aa	Aa	3 39	5 53	....
11¼	Habrough	7 40	1023	1123	3 50	6 4	....
13	Brocklesby ..... arr.	7 44	1027	....	3 53	6 8	....
—	820 Hull B ...... dep.	6 27	9 12	10 7	2 37	4 42	5 12
—	820 New Holland "	7 5	9b50	1047	3 20	5 20	6 0
—	Brocklesby ...... dep.	7 45	1031	11 6	3 54	6 9	6 19
17¾	Barnetby ...... arr.	7 53	1039	1134	4 3	6 17	6 28
	Barnetby ...... dep.	7 57	1040	1148	4 10	6 20	7 5
21¼	Howsham	8 5	1048	....	....	6 27	7 13
23¾	North Kelsey	8 9	1052	....	4 25	6 31	7 17
25¼	Moortown A	8 14	1056	12 0	4 29	6 35	7 21
26¾	Holton-le-Moor	8 19	11 0	....	....	6 39	7 25
29½	Claxby and Usselby	8 25	11 7	....	4 37	6 45	7 32
32½	Market Rasen	8 32	1115	1212	4 44	6 53	7 40
36¼	Wickenby	8 40	1123	....	4 52	7 1	7 48
37¾	Snelland ....[by	8 45	1128	....	4 57	....	7 53
41	Langworth, for Wrag-	8 53	1134	....	5 3	7 11	7 59
42½	Reepham (Lincs) 754	9 0	1138	....	5 7	7 15	8 3
47¼	Lincoln C 732, arr.	9 10	1148	1238	5 17	7 25	8 15

NOTES.

A Station for Caistor (2¾ miles).
Aa Takes up for Habrough and beyond on giving notice at the Station.
B Corporation Pier (by Boat).
b Departs at 10 5 mrn. on Thursdays.
C L. N. E.
Dd Stops when required.
F Fridays only.
Kk Stops to set down from Barnetby or beyond on notice being given to the Guard at Barnetby.

May 1944

LINCOLN, BARNETBY, and CLEETHORPES

Miles	Week Days only	mrn D	mrn	mrn D	aft D	aft D
—	Lincoln .... dep	6 15	..	8 42	5 7	8 42
4¾	Reepham (Lincs.)	6 27	..	8 50	5 15	8 50
6½	Langworth, for Wragby	Aa	..	8 54	5 19	8 54
9¼	Snelland	6 37	..	9 0	5 25	9 0
11	Wickenby	6 41	..	9 4	5 29	9 4
14¾	Market Rasen	6A53	..	9 13	5 38	9 13
17¾	Claxby and Usselby	6 58	..	9 18	5 43	9 21
20½	Holton-le-Moor	7 3	..	9 23	5 48	9 26
22	Moortown, for Caistor	7 8	..	9 27	5 52	9 30
23½	North Kelsey	7 12	..	9 31	5 56	9 34
25½	Howsham	7 17	..	9 35	6 0	9 38
29½	Barnetby ...... arr	7 26	—	9 43	6 7	9 46
	Barnetby ...... dep	7 29	9 58	10 7	6 15	9 51
34½	Brocklesby ...... arr	7 37	..	10 15	6S23	..
41¾	68 New Holland .. arr	8B48	..	10B42	7B46	10B38
44½	68 Hull (CorptionPier) "	9 30	..	11 25	8U15	..
—	Brocklesby ...... dep	7 38	..	10 16	6S24	..
35¾	Habrough	7 43	..	10 22	6 27	10 3
39¾	Stallingborough	7 50	..	10 29	..	..
40¾	Healing	7 53	..	10 32	..	..
42	Great Coates	7 57	..	10 36	..	..
44	Grimsby Town	8 2	1019	10 41	6 40	10 16
45	Grimsby Docks	8 9	1029	10 50	6 49	10 25
45¾	New Clee	..	..	10 55	6 53	..
47¼	Cleethorpes ..... arr	8 19	1037	10 59	6 57	10 33

Week Days only	mrn D	mrn D	aft F	aft D
Cleethorpes ..... dep	6 55	10 5	2J20	5 22
New Clee	6 59	..	..	5 26
Grimsby Docks	7 6	1014	2J33	5A35
Grimsby Town	7 14	1019	2J41	5 46
Great Coates	7 19	..	12J51	5 52
Healing	7 22	..	1J30	5 56
Stallingborough	7 26	..	1J33	6 0
Habrough	7 34	1034	2J57	6V10
Brocklesby ...... arr	7 37	1037	..	6 13
68 Hull (C'n.Pier)* dep	..	9 10	1 15	4 30
68 New Holland... "	6B30	9B53	2 33	5B10
Brocklesby ...... dep	7 38	1038	2 52	6 14
Barnetby ...... arr	7 46	1047	3 0	6 23
Barnetby ...... dep	7 51	1054	3 15	6 29
Howsham	7 58	11 1	3 22	6 36
North Kelsey	8 1	11 4	3 25	6 40
Moortown, for Caistor	8 5	11 8	3 29	6 45
Holton-le Moor	8 9	1112	3 33	6 49
Claxby and Usselby	8 14	1117	3 38	6 54
Market Rasen	8 22	1125	3 46	7A 5
Wickenby	8 29	1132	3 53	7 12
Snelland	8 32	1135	3 56	7 15
Langworth, for Wragby	8 38	1141	4 2	7 21
Reepham (Lincs.)	8 42	1145	4 6	7 25
Lincoln .... arr	8 50	1155	4 16	7 37

Aa Calls 6 31 mrn. when required to set down on notice being given to Guard at Lincoln
A Arr. 5 mins. *earlier*
B Change at Habrough
D Through Train between Lincoln and Cleethorpes
F Through Train New Holland to Lincoln
J Change at Barnetby
S Saturdays only
U Commences 10th April
V Arr. 4 mins. *earlier*

* The times shown leaving Hull are those at which the Ferry leaves the Corporation Pier, and passengers having to book must present themselves at the Booking Office in Nelson Street at least three minutes before times advertised for departure of Ferry (see * note Table 69)

LINCOLN, BARNETBY and CLEETHORPES

Miles	Week Days only		am	am	am Except Saturdays — Through Train Derby (Mid.) (dep 8 12 am) to Cleethorpes (Table 56)	am Saturdays only	pm Except Saturdays	pm Saturdays only	pm	pm Through Train Derby (Mid.) (dep 6 23 pm) to Cleethorpes (Table 56)	pm Except Saturdays	pm Saturdays only
	Lincoln (St. Marks)	dep			10 16	10 16				8 16		
—	Lincoln (Central	„	5 50	8 31			1 15	1 15	5 17		9 12	9 12
4¾	Reepham (Lincs.)		5 58	8 39			1 23	1 23	5 25		9 20	9 20
6½	Langworth			8 42			1 26	1 26	5 28			
9½	Snelland		6 5	8 47			1 31	1 31	5 33		9 27	9 27
11	Wickenby		6 9	8 51			1 35	1 35	5 37		9 31	9 31
14¾	Market Rasen		6e20	9d 2	10 36	10 36	1 42	1 42	5 45	8 36	9 39	9 39
20¼	Holton-le-Moor		6 28	9 11			1 51	1 51	5 54		9 47	9 47
22	Moortown		6 32	9 15			1 55	1 55	5 58		9 51	9 51
23¼	North Kelsey		6 36	9 18			1 58	1 58	6 1		9 55	9 55
25¼	Howsham		6 40	9 22				2 2	6 5		9 59	9 59
29¼	Barnetby	arr	6 48	9 30	10 54	10 54	2 10	2 10	6 13	8 54	10 7	10 7
		dep	6 49	9 34	10 58	10 58	2 12	2 12	6 17	8 56	10 8	10 8
34¼	Brocklesby		6 57				2 19	2 19	6 24			
—	Habrough	arr	7 0	9 43	11 8	11 8	2 22	2 22	6 28	9 5	10 18	1018
—	58 New Holland (Town)	arr	8A 1	10 48	11 43	11 43	3 28	3 28	7 48	9 31		
—	58 Hull (Corporation Pier)	„	8A35	11 25	12 25	12 25	4 0	4 0	8 20	10 0		
35¼	Habrough	dep	7 1	9 44	11 9	11 9	2 23	2 23	6 29	9 6	10 20	1020
39¼	Stallingborough		7 7	9 50	11 15	11 15	2 29					
40¾	Healing		7 10	9 53	11 17	11 17	2 32	2 31		9 14		
42	Great Coates		7 14	9 57			2 36					
44	Grimsby Town	arr	7 19	10 2	11 24	11 24	2 41	2 38	6 44	9 21	10 33	1031
		dep		10 5	11 28	11 28	2 44	2 41	6 49	9 24		1037
45	Grimsby Docks	arr		10 7	11 30	11 30	2 47	2 44	6 52			
45¾	New Clee	„					2 53	2 50	6E57			
47¼	Cleethorpes	„		10 17	11 40	11 40	3 0	2 57	7 4	9 34		1047

A On Saturdays arr New Holland (Town) 8 39 and Hull (Corporation Pier) 9 25 am

c Arr 3 minutes *earlier*
d Arr 4 minutes *earlier*
E Except Saturdays
e Arr 5 minutes *earlier*

Q Change at Habrough and Barnetb
R Change at Barnetby
S Saturdays only

September 1964

May 1985

Lincoln, Grimsby and Cleethorpes

Miles	Miles		A		BHX	BHX	C				D	C			C			
—	—	Crewe 80 d				0600		0720			0810		0920			1120		
—	—	Derby 80 d			0650	0735		0845			1005		1105			1305		
0	—	Nottingham d			0721	0808		0924			1033		1140		1234	1339		
3¼	—	Carlton d			0727	0814		0930			1039		1146		1240	1345		
5¼	—	Burton Joyce d			0731	0818		0934			1043		1150		1244	1349		
7¼	—	Lowdham d			0736	0823		0939			1048		1155		1249	1354		
9¾	—	Thurgarton d			0741	0828		0944					1159		1253			
11	—	Bleasby d			0744	0831		0947			1053		1202		1257	1359		
12¾	—	Fiskerton d			0748	0835		0951					1206		1301			
13¼	—	Rolleston d			0750	0837		0953					1209					
17¼	—	Newark Castle d			0757	0844		1000			1102		1216		1308	1408		
—	0	London Kings Cross ⊖ 26 d		0532			0804					1004						1250
—	76½	Peterborough 26 d		0648			0905					1105						1305
—	120	Newark North Gate d		0735			0950					1150						1418
22¼	125	Collingham d		0743	0805	0852		1008			1110		1224		1316	1416		1426
25	127¾	Swinderby d			0810	0857		1013			1115		1229		1321			1431
29¾	132½	Hykeham d			0818	0905		1021			1123		1237		1328			1439
33	135¾	Lincoln St.Marks a		0758	0824	0911	1011	1027			1129	1211	1243		1334	1431		1445
—	—	d	0543b	0800			1013					1213						1446
48	150¾	Market Rasen d	0611c	0818			1031					1231						1505
62¾	165½	Barnetby 29 d	0638c	0839			1053					1252						1526
69	171¾	Habrough 29 d	0650	0849			1103					1302						1536
77	179¾	Grimsby Town 29 d	0712	0904			1118					1317						1551
78	180¾	Grimsby Docks 29 d																
80¼	183	Cleethorpes 29 a	0724	0914			1127					1327						1600

			C					C	SX	SO		E	P S GC 125 Ø			C SO	C SX	
Crewe 80 d		1220e		1320	1420	1520						1620		1830				
Derby 80 d		1410		1504	1605	1648			1720	1720		1805		2012				2105
Nottingham d		1447		1536	1634	1720			1752	1800		1840		2040				2141
Carlton d		1453		1542	1640	1726			1758	1806		1846		2046				2147
Burton Joyce d		1457		1546	1644	1730			1802	1810		1850		2050				2151
Lowdham d		1502		1551	1649	1735			1807	1815		1855		2055				2156
Thurgarton d				1555	1654	1739			1811	1819		1859						2200
Bleasby d		1507		1558	1657	1742			1814	1822		1902						2203
Fiskerton d		1511		1602	1701	1746			1818	1826		1906						2207
Rolleston d				1605	1703				1821	1829								
Newark Castle d		1518		1612	1710	1752			1827	1835		1914		2107				2214
London Kings Cross ⊖ 26 d			1404					1637			1730f		1818			2004	2004	2050
Peterborough 26 d			1505					1705					1922			2105	2105	2145
Newark North Gate d			1600					1808			1900		2001			2149	2149	2226
Collingham d		1526		1620	1718	1800		1816	1835	1843	1908	1922		2115		2157	2157	2235
Swinderby d		1531		1625	1723	1805			1840	1848		1927		2120				2240
Hykeham d		1539		1632	1731	1813			1848	1856		1935		2127				2247
Lincoln St.Marks a		1545	1621	1638	1737	1819		1831	1854	1902	1923	1941	2020	2133		2212	2212	2253
d			1623		1738			1833					2022				2216	
Market Rasen d			1641		1757			1851					2040				2234	
Barnetby 29 d			1702		1818			1912					2059				2255	
Habrough 29 d			1712		1827			1922					2108				2305	
Grimsby Town 29 d			1727		1843			1937					2124				2320	
Grimsby Docks 29 d																		
Cleethorpes 29 a			1736		1852			1946					2133				2329	

A From Manchester Piccadilly dep. 0210 (Table 29)
C First and Second Class
D From Birmingham New Street dep. 0907 (Table 56)
E From Birmingham New Street dep. 1655 (1650 Saturdays until 29 September) (Table 56)
G **The Humber-Lincs Executive**
J From Chester dep. 1915 (Table 83)
b Lincoln Central
c Arr. Market Rasen 0602, Barnetby 0633
e Change at Derby
f Saturdays dep. 1733

Sunday times are below picture 11.

LINCOLN ST. MARKS

II.   This diagram from 1981 shows the destinations of all the routes radiating from Lincoln. A link south from Boultham Junction to the Newark line was provided later - see the next map caption. (The Railway Magazine)

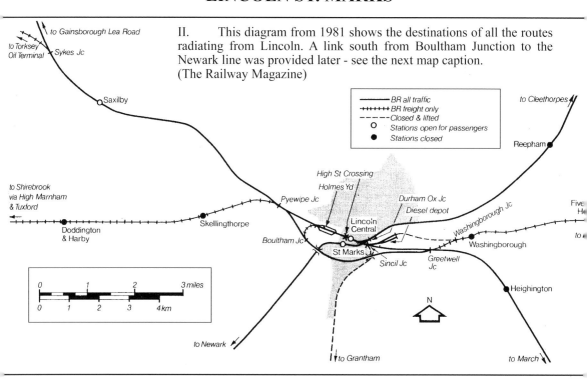

1.   The east end is seen in about 1930, when there were two platforms, but four tracks. The centre two were used for storage of stock and were separated by a row of iron columns. The gates overlapped when across the road. A single tram track was in the road from 1882 until 1929, horses being in action until 1904 when overhead wires came into use. (Stations UK)

2.   Four of the staff of over 40 pose towards the end of the one horse power transport era. The oval window design was incorporated into later motor van designs. The station was built by the MR in 1846 and a refreshment and a dining room were added in 1849. (P.Laming coll.)

3.   The splendid Grecian columns are pictured in 1965 and they avoided demolition. They survive, having been incorporated into a shopping centre, together with the square pilasters. (R.J.Essery/R.S.Carpenter)

III.   The 1933 survey at 6ins to 1 mile has the LMS route to Newark lower left and its station to the left of the High Street. The suffix "St. Marks" was used for it from 29th September 1950 until 12th May 1985, when a curve was opened between the top of this caption and Boultham Junction. All trains thereafter used the ex-LNER one which is shown to the right of the High Street and was termed "Central" between those dates. The curve between Ballast Holes (left) and Cow Paddle (right) was a GNR/GCR joint venture in 1882 to form a bypass, but it was closed in 1983. Top left is the Gainsborough line and below it is the Chesterfield route. On the right border, from the top: Grimsby, Boston and Sleaford, with the Grantham route at the lower border. Below Brayford Bridge, on the left of the right page, is the ex-GNR engine shed, which was in use until 1964. It is above the ex-GCR goods shed. The ex-MR engine shed is further east, above Pelham Street Junction. It can be seen in picture 17.

4.   The overall roof vanished in 1957 and scaffold canopies were provided, these lasting until closure in 1985. One of the two low servicing platforms can be seen to the right of the coach. (Lens of Sutton coll.)

5.   All four gates were recorded on 10th November 1965, but the adjacent goods yard had closed on 3rd May of that year. It was ex-MR; the GCR yard was further east, close to Kesteven Street - see map IV. It became a coal concentration depot. The two large poster boards were on the east side of the High Street. Conventional traffic lights were fitted on 1956, but are out of view. (R.J.Essery/R.S.Carpenter)

6. Class 114 cars E50026 and E56013 are pictured on 23rd August 1978. At that time the entire fleet of 50 class 114 units was allocated to Lincoln. The signal box controlling the crossing was called Lincoln Roundhouse. It had a gate wheel plus a 6-lever frame. It opened in 1874 and closed on 19th July 2008, by which time it had become a listed structure. (P.D.Shannon)

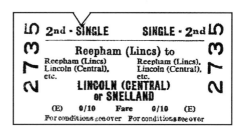

7.　　　No. 47380 passes Lincoln coal concentration depot, located just east of St. Marks station, with the 08.31 Colwick to Lindsey Refinery empty oil tank train on 13th April 1983. Three hopper wagons await unloading, apparently carrying different grades of coal. The coal depot closed soon after the date of this photograph, there being insufficient traffic to warrant a Speedlink Coal service. (P.D.Shannon)

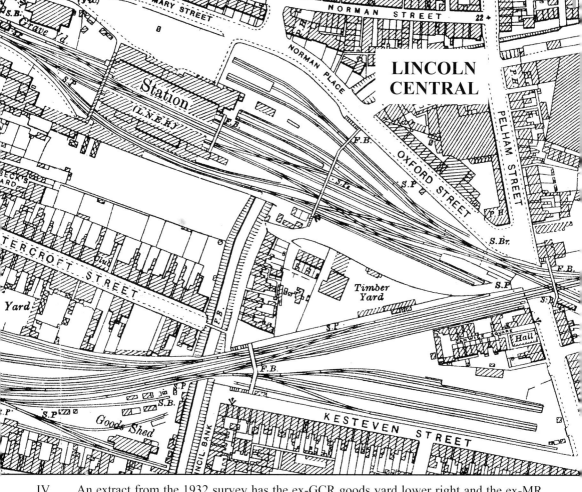

IV. An extract from the 1932 survey has the ex-GCR goods yard lower right and the ex-MR running lines from St. Marks are the lower pair, ending at Pelham Street. Central station is at the top. The level crossing was known as "Durham Ox", after the public house north of it.

8. A train bound for Cleethorpes waits to depart on 8th June 1926. LNER no. 5700 was a class D7 4-4-0, built for the MS&LR. The bridge carries a public footpath, with no access to the platforms. It had a companion to the south, over the St. Marks lines. (H.C.Casserley)

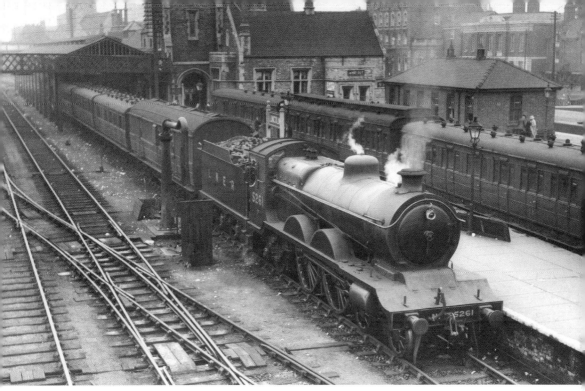

9.	Viewed from the public footbridge is LNER no. 5261, alongside the water column. This is a class C4 4-4-2, a type introduced in 1903 by the GCR. There were eight platforms, this being no. 5. Bay platforms nos 1-4 are to the right. (R.M.Casserley coll.)

10.	The station footbridge is featured in this westward view from about 1950, as an express speeds through. There is fine cast iron tracery at both platforms and no snow on either. No. 6 is on the left, this being an island platform. The following were in use in 2013 (coach lengths are in brackets): 3(5), 4(3), 5(7), 6 and 7 (both 7). (Stations UK)

11.	The bay platforms were used by trains bound for Grimsby, Skegness, Bolton, Sleaford and Grantham, plus parcel traffic. Durham Ox crossing suffered severe traffic congestion and required four men to move the gates. Thus an avoiding line was opened in 1882 and it is marked MARCH & DONCASTER on map III. Class B1 4-6-0 no. 61326 is seen from Pelham Street Box on 21st May 1956. (B.W.L.Brooksbank)

May 1985

Lincoln, Grimsby and Cleethorpes											Sundays		
	C			C			S C 125 Ø					J	
Crewe ....80 d	....	....	....	....	....	1615	....	....	1722	1825	....	1943	....
Derby ....80 d	..	1430	..	..	..	1740	..	..	1900	2006	..	2120	..
Nottingham ....d	....	1515	....	....	....	1821	....	....	1940	2101	....	2150	....
Carlton ....d	..	1521	..	..	..	1827	..	..	1946	2107	..	2156	..
Burton Joyce ....d	....	1525	....	....	....	1831	....	....	1950	2111	....	2200	....
Lowdham ....d	..	1530	..	..	..	1836	..	..	1955	2116	..	2205	..
Thurgarton ....d	....	1534	....	....	....	1841	....	....	1959	2120	....	2209	....
Bleasby ....d	..	1537	..	..	..	1844	..	..	2002	2123	..	2212	..
Fiskerton ....d	....	1541	....	....	....	1848	....	....	2006	2127	....	2216	....
Rolleston ....d	..	..	..	..	..	..	..	..	..	..	..	..	..
Newark Castle ....d	....	1548	....	....	....	1854	....	....	2013	2134	....	2223	....
London Kings Cross ....Ꝋ 26 d	1204	..	1404	..	1637	..	1733	1818	..	2004	..	2050	..
Peterborough ....26 d	1310	....	1510	....	1705	....	....	1922	....	2105	....	2145	....
Newark North Gate ....d	1408	....	1556	1615	....	1820	1907	2001	....	2149	....	2235	....
Collingham ....d	..	..	1556	1623	..	..	1915	1920	2022	2157	..	2244	..
Swinderby ....d	..	..	1601	..	..	..	1920	2027	2202	..	..	..	..
Hykeham ....d	....	....	1608	..	....	....	1928	2035	2210	....	....	....	....
Lincoln St.Marks ....a	1429	1614	1638	..	1841	..	1934	2020	2041	2216	..	2259	..
...............................d	1431	..	1640	..	1843	..	..	2022	..	..	..	..	..
Market Rasen ....d	1449	..	1658	..	1901	..	..	2040	..	..	..	..	..
Barnetby ....29 d	1510	..	1719	..	1922	..	..	2059	..	..	..	..	..
Habrough ....29 d	1520	..	1729	..	1932	..	..	2108	..	..	..	..	..
Grimsby Town ....29 d	1535	..	1744	..	1947	..	..	2124	..	..	..	..	..
Grimsby Docks ....29 d	..	..	..	..	..	..	..	..	..	..	..	..	..
Cleethorpes ....29 a	1544	....	1754	....	1956	....	....	2133	....	....	....	....	....

12.   An eastward panorama from 6th June 1969 has the public footbridge largely obscuring the new road bridge. Pelham Street Flyover was built in 1958 after years of frustration by road users, but the Durham Ox itself had to be demolished. The white abutments are evident. Platform 8 had been on the right, but it had lost its track by that time. (H.C.Casserley)

13.   The prospective passenger's perspective was photographed on 20th September 1975. To harmonise with the town, the GNR forgot its cheap policy and indulged in grey bricks with stone dressings, several pointed arches, Tudor gables and a Baronial tower, with circular windows. (D.A.Thompson)

14.　　The new bridge is seen from the footbridge on 7th October 1976, as no. 08209 does a local trip working. Just beyond the far end of the train is the crossing featured in pictures 16 and 17. (T.Heavyside)

15.   The canopy stanchions have gone, but the other architectural details still remain to be enjoyed, along with the Church of St. Mary le Wigford beyond. Two class 114s, a class 101 DMU plus an 08 shunter rest on 20th July 1984. (J.Whitehouse)

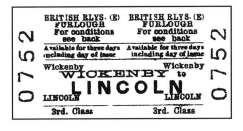

16.   Pelham Street signal box is on the right as no. 37042 approaches the station on 7th October 1976, with steel from Scunthorpe. The GNR box was the third here and its 100-lever frame came into use in 1874. Closure came on 19th July 2008. Rustons had extensive works in the city, their output including small locomotives, excavators and much agricultural equipment. Other notable producers were Clayton Dewandre and Smith-Clayton Forge. (T.Heavyside)

17.   A different angle from the same footbridge on 28th July 1979 includes the gates on the Sleaford line and the nearby Sincil Junction Box. The line curving to the left of it runs to Boston. No. E50001 is working from Cleethorpes to Newark and has just run over the junction for the shed branch and its next stop will be St. Marks. The first shed was built by the GCR and had last been used for steam locomotives in 1939, but a new one was built for diesel units in 1958. (T.Heavyside)

REEPHAM LINCS.

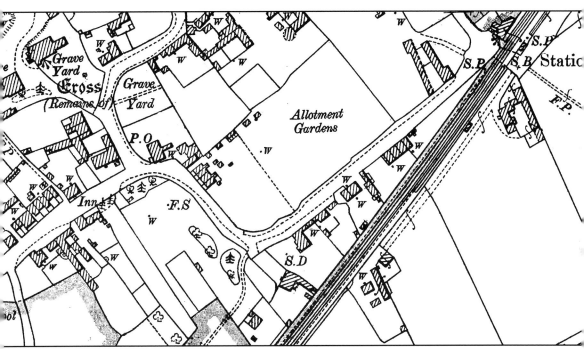

V.   Before reaching here, trains once ran past Clayton's Siding, where there was a 14-lever signal box from 1883 to about 1925. Then came Monks Abbey Box (18 levers), in use from around 1889 until 23rd September 1984. The map is from 1907 and shows the close proximity of the station to the village. The population was 387 in 1901 and about 1250 at the end of 2013. There are also recent oil wells in the parish.

18.   A 2-8-0 is running north sometime in 1961 and on the left is the end of the goods yard, which closed on 30th December 1963. The suffix LINCS was added on 1st July 1923 and passenger service ceased on 1st November 1965. The opening date was sometime in 1849. (Stations UK)

19.   A northward view from 1961 includes the MS&LR 20-lever box, which functioned from 1890 until 20th May 1990. Beyond it is the connection to the goods siding. (Stations UK)

2nd   PRIVILEGE   PRIVILEGE   -2nd
        SINGLE   SINGLE
1523   Reepham (Lincs.) to   1523
        Reepham (Lincs.)   Reepham (Lincs.)
        Lincoln (Cent.), etc.   Lincoln (Cent.), etc.
        LINCOLN (Central) or
        SNELLAND
        (E)   0/4   Fare   0/4   (E)
        For conditions see over   For conditions see over

0742   L. N. E. R.   L. N. E. R.   0742
        EVENING EXCURSION   EVENING EXCURSION
        CLEETHORPES   REEPHAM (LINCS.)
        TO   TO
        REEPHAM (LINCS.)   CLEETHORPES
        Valid as per Bills.   Valid as per Bills.
        THIRD   EVENING EXC.   THIRD
        For conditions   2153   For conditions
        see back   CLEETHORPES   see back

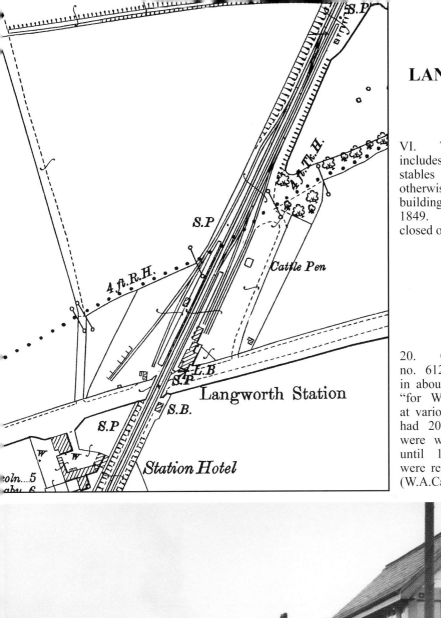

LANGWORTH

VI. The 1907 survey includes the essential stables behind the inn, otherwise all are railway buildings, opened during 1849. The goods yard closed on 15th June 1964.

20. Class B1 4-6-0 no. 61279 was recorded in about 1955. The suffix "for Wragby" was used at various times. The box had 20 levers and they were worked from 1890 until 1990, when they were replaced by a panel. (W.A.Camwell/SLS coll.)

21.	The massive gate partially obscures the foot crossing in this 1961 northward view. The black iron parts on the right were linked to the gate wheel in the box. Few platforms were totally devoid of shelters, except on this line. (Stations UK)

22.	The same view in 1994 reveals elimination of all notable historical architectural features, even the bay window. The last passengers had turned their backs on 1st November 1965 and neglect of the area began. (C.L.Caddy)

SNELLAND

VII. The 1907 edition features a modest goods yard, which lasted until 30th December 1963. The station opening date is uncertain, but was during 1849.

23. Two pictures from 1961 present the rural but flat landscape. Here we look south, but only a fragment of a siding can be seen as a DMU with cats whiskers arrives. (Stations UK)

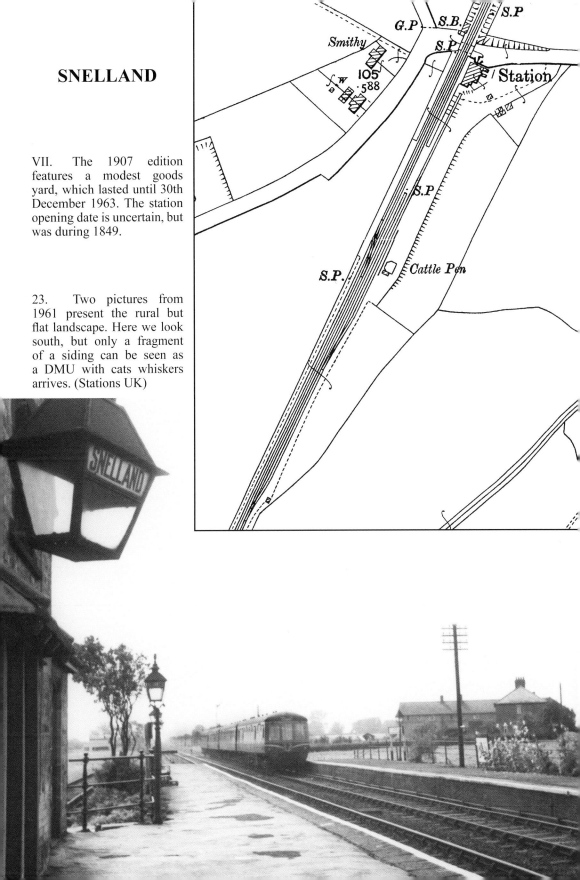

24.   No shelters were provided, as there were few passengers. As at the adjacent stations, trains ceased to call on 1st November 1965. The signal box of 1890 had 23 levers and was functioning until 5th November 1989. (Stations UK)

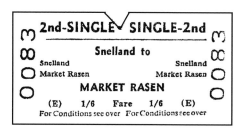

WICKENBY

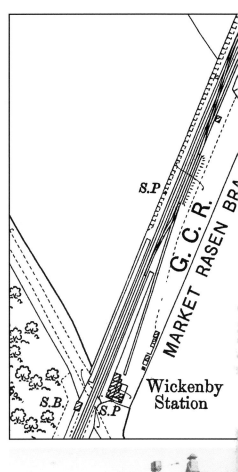

Wickenby
Station

25.   The MS&LR box was completed in about 1890 and had a 20-lever frame. This was replaced by a panel in 1990, which was still in use in 2013. (P.Laming coll.)

VIII.   Another 1907 extract and this one shows the signal box to be backing onto rare Lincolnshire woodland. The station opened on 1st February 1849 and was 71ft above sea level.

26.   Beyond the right platform is the goods yard, which closed on 30th December 1963. Seen in 1961, the platforms were last used on 1st November 1965. Again, no shelters were provided. (Stations UK)

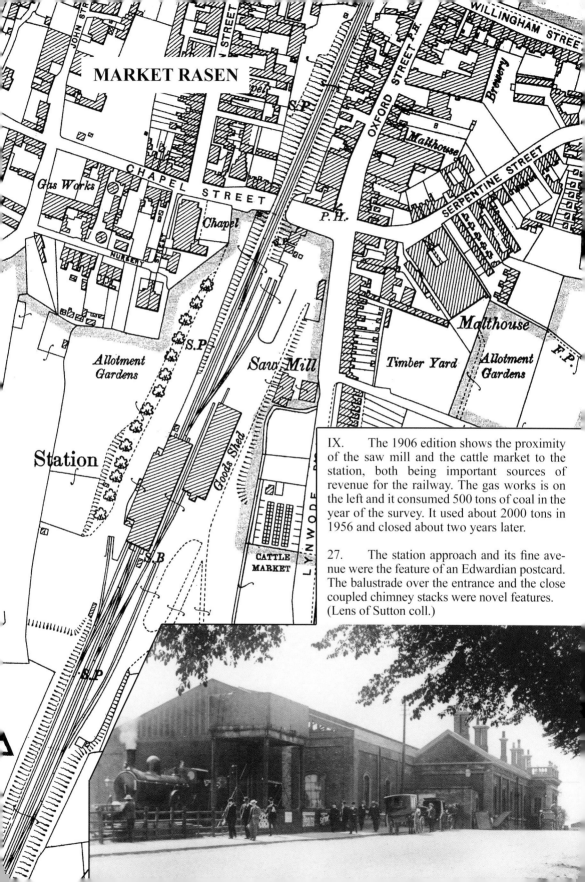

MARKET RASEN

IX. The 1906 edition shows the proximity of the saw mill and the cattle market to the station, both being important sources of revenue for the railway. The gas works is on the left and it consumed 500 tons of coal in the year of the survey. It used about 2000 tons in 1956 and closed about two years later.

27. The station approach and its fine avenue were the feature of an Edwardian postcard. The balustrade over the entrance and the close coupled chimney stacks were novel features. (Lens of Sutton coll.)

28.   Another early record reveals the comfort provided for passengers here, although there were only 2188 residents in 1901. This increased to just 2300 by 1961.
(P.Laming coll.)

29.   We have seen the water tank before, but not the massive goods shed, the roof of which is on the right. We have no date for the station roof loss, but the picture of this DMU arriving from the north is from 1961.
(Stations UK)

30.	A view in the other direction on the same occasion shows the DMU departing with a van in tow. The points are to the three short sidings, one of which had a wharf. (Stations UK)

31.	The 15.19 Cleethorpes to Newark was recorded on 28th July 1979, along with part of the end wall of the original station. The MS&LR box of about 1890 had 29 levers and closed on 22nd March 1981. It was later moved to the GCR for preservation at Quorn & Woodhouse station. (T.Heavyside)

32.   The station was unstaffed from 29th June 1969 to 5th October 1970, but this picture from 22nd June 1994 shows a return to normality, although two chimney pots are missing. (C.L.Caddy)

33.   No. 66170 is running north on 6th March 2009, by which time both platforms were recorded as suitable for just three coaches. This was then the only station open on the 29½ miles from Lincoln to Barnetby. (R.Geach)

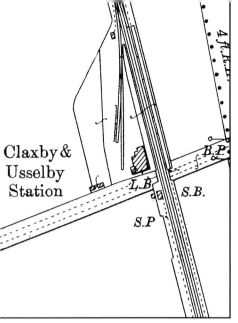

Claxby &
Usselby
Station

CLAXBY AND USSELBY

X.   The station opened with the line and was named just USSELBY. It was as shown on this 1907 map from 1st July 1897. The former was over a mile distant and the latter was nearby, but smaller. It later had a change of spelling, becoming Ulceby.

34.   An early postcard presents the fine eastern elevation, but there was no provision for shelter on the opposite platform. The domestic accommodation must have been generous. (P.Laming coll.)

35.   Both passenger and freight services were withdrawn on 7th March 1960. The premises are seen in the following year, together with part of the loading gauge. The 1890 signal box was behind the camera. Its 20-lever frame was in use until 22nd April 1989. (Stations UK)

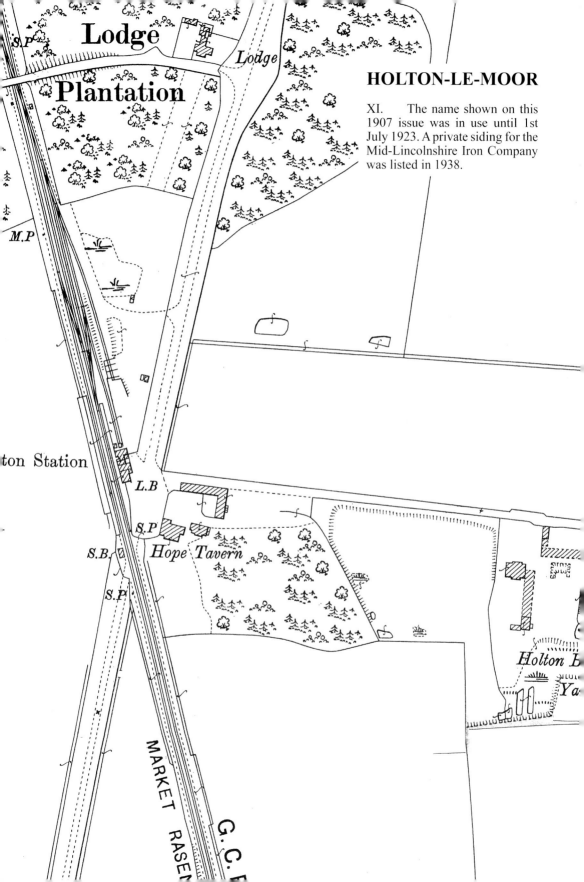

Lodge

Plantation

Lodge

S.P

M.P

ton Station

L.B

S.P

S.B

S.P

Hope Tavern

MARKET RASEN

G.C.R

Holton B

Ya

HOLTON-LE-MOOR

XI.   The name shown on this 1907 issue was in use until 1st July 1923. A private siding for the Mid-Lincolnshire Iron Company was listed in 1938.

36.   A photograph from about 1930 includes the A46 and the standard station design used on the route. The local population numbered 178 in 1881 and 163 in 1901. (Stations UK)

37.   No. 47292 passes through with the 08.30 Humber to Kingsbury petroleum train on 12th April 1983. This flow still operated in 2013 but with 30-wagon trainloads instead of the modest load of eleven tanks pictured here. The station closed to goods in June 1964 and to passengers on 1st November 1965, but the signal box remained in use in 2013. (P.D.Shannon)

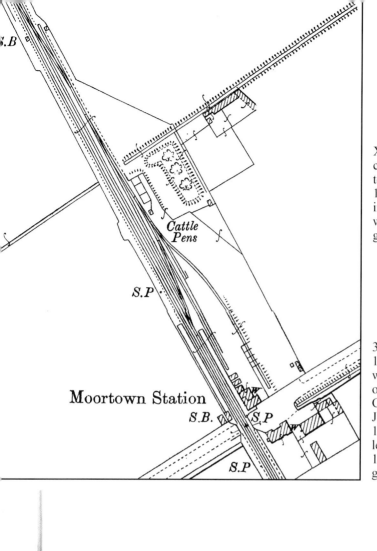

MOORTOWN

XII.   The station served a tiny community almost a mile away, to the west. The road on this 1907 survey became the B1025 in 1919. The suffix "for Caistor" was used at times. By 1938, the goods yard had a 5-ton crane.

38.   One photograph from 1961 will suffice, as all structures were replicas of those found at other small stations on the route. Closure to goods was on 15th June 1964 and to passengers on 1st November 1965. The 24-lever box lasted until 16th April 1989 and was preserved in the goods yard. (Stations UK)

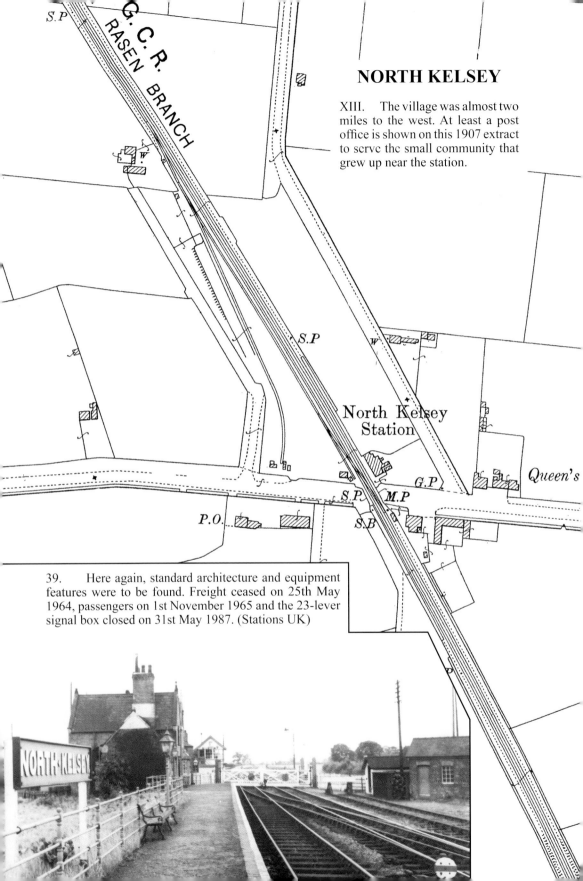

NORTH KELSEY

XIII. The village was almost two miles to the west. At least a post office is shown on this 1907 extract to serve the small community that grew up near the station.

39. Here again, standard architecture and equipment features were to be found. Freight ceased on 25th May 1964, passengers on 1st November 1965 and the 23-lever signal box closed on 31st May 1987. (Stations UK)

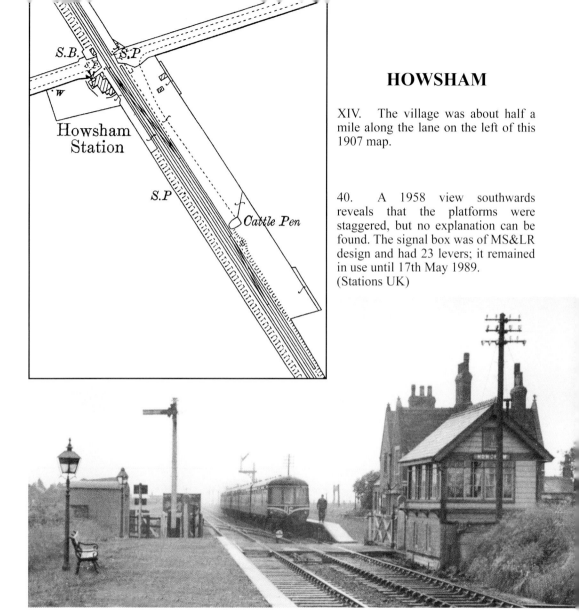

HOWSHAM

XIV. The village was about half a mile along the lane on the left of this 1907 map.

40. A 1958 view southwards reveals that the platforms were staggered, but no explanation can be found. The signal box was of MS&LR design and had 23 levers; it remained in use until 17th May 1989. (Stations UK)

41. A 1961 record includes coal traffic in the yard, which closed on 30th December 1963. Passenger trains called until 1st November 1965. (Stations UK)

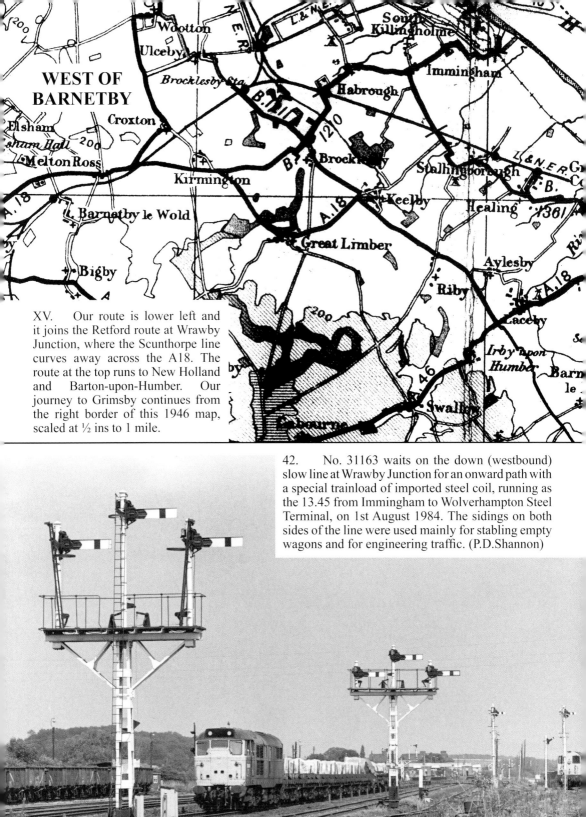

WEST OF BARNETBY

XV.   Our route is lower left and it joins the Retford route at Wrawby Junction, where the Scunthorpe line curves away across the A18. The route at the top runs to New Holland and Barton-upon-Humber. Our journey to Grimsby continues from the right border of this 1946 map, scaled at ½ ins to 1 mile.

42.   No. 31163 waits on the down (westbound) slow line at Wrawby Junction for an onward path with a special trainload of imported steel coil, running as the 13.45 from Immingham to Wolverhampton Steel Terminal, on 1st August 1984. The sidings on both sides of the line were used mainly for stabling empty wagons and for engineering traffic. (P.D.Shannon)

43.   No. 60038 is at Wrawby Junction on 23rd February 1996, with empty tankers. The box was completed by the GCR in 1916 and was fitted with 137 levers. It became a listed structure and was the third largest box in Britain. First was Shrewsbury Severn Bridge (180) and second was Stafford No. 5 (150). All three were still in use in 2013. (J.Whitehouse)

44.   Another signal array can be enjoyed as no. 153365 runs by on 20th June 2003, while working the 16.03 Grimsby Town to Newark North Gate service. The box is in line with the signal post. (D.H.Mitchell)

BARNETBY

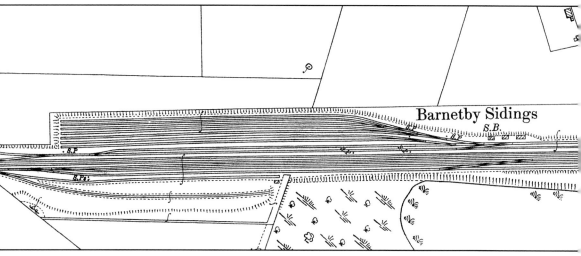

Barnetby Sidings
S.B.

XVI.   The 1906 edition is shown at 20ins to 1 mile, with much marshland south of the railway. The village was known as Barnetby-le-Wold and housed 1144 souls in 1901. The group of sidings on the left page were used for trains of spent ballast in later years.

45.   The east end of the station is seen from a public footbridge and Station Box is included. This had 39 levers and was in use from about 1889 until 1914. The crane was rated at 5 tons. (P.Laming coll.)

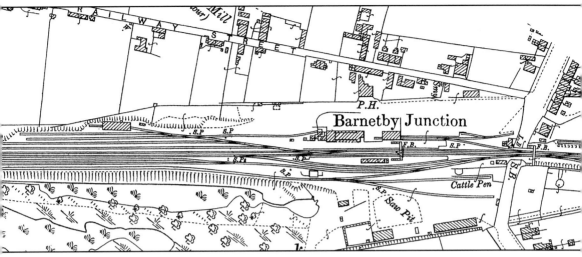

Barnetby Junction

46.   A steam-free postcard includes the subsequent East Box. The population had risen to 1593 by 2001. The oil lamps demanded much labour at each end of the day. (Lens of Sutton coll.)

47.   Although not many lived nearby, the station was often busy as a junction. The east ends of the marshalling yards are included in this view of no. 263. This was a class C4 4-4-2. (Lens of Sutton coll.)

48.   A record from 1st June 1957 includes the LNER's favourite lighting form, a white globe. They were out of use for five years during World War II. Note that the footbridge had lost its roof. (H.C.Casserley)

49.   A westward panorama from 17th April 1961 includes the water tower and West Box, in the distance. This had 72 levers and was in use from 1916 until 30th December 1973. The goods shed is on the right, freight traffic ceased on 6th July 1964. There was a 5-ton crane in the yard in 1938. (B.W.L.Brooksbank)

50.   Additional lighting had been provided by 27th July 1979, when no. 55006 was pictured with a Kings Cross to Cleethorpes service. The bullhead rails were near the end of their careers. (T.Heavyside)

51.   DMUs flank the facilities for gentlemen on 13th March 1989. At platform 1 is the 10.10 Birmingham New Street to Cleethorpes and at No. 2 is the 11.31 Sheffield to Cleethorpes. (D.H.Mitchell)

52.   It is 16th March 1992 and no. 158772 waits at the signal. The buildings had been demolished in February and the northern end of the Lincolnshire Wolds is on the left. The line in the right background led to the seven up sidings. (M.J.Stretton)

53. No. 66220 runs through on 8th May 2003. There were four running lines and south of them were two reception roads and five down sidings. Parts of the small shelters are evident. (M.Dart)

54. The main building had been converted as offices for NR. This is the north elevation on 30th November 2006. The suffix "for Humberside Airport" had been brought into use by that time. (A.C.Hartless)

55.   No. 66164 enters the station on 22nd August 2012 with the 11.40 Humber to Kingsbury petroleum train, a good example of a modern freight service, weighing in at around 2750 tonnes gross. The 72-lever Barnetby East signal box is a GCR design, which opened in 1914 and was still in use in 2013. (P.D.Shannon)

EAST OF
BARNETBY

56.   Quadruple track was available between Barnetby and Brocklesby when this photograph was taken on 30th April 1986, but the down goods line was later lifted. Nos. 37002 and 37119 were hauling a load of iron ore from Immingham to Scunthorpe, near the site of Melton Ross Siding Box; its 96-lever frame served from 1911 to 1982. Melton Ross had 187 residents in 2001. The quarry produces lime from the chalk evident on the right. Singleton Birch was established in 1815 and grew steadily to the extent shown. (J.Whitehouse)

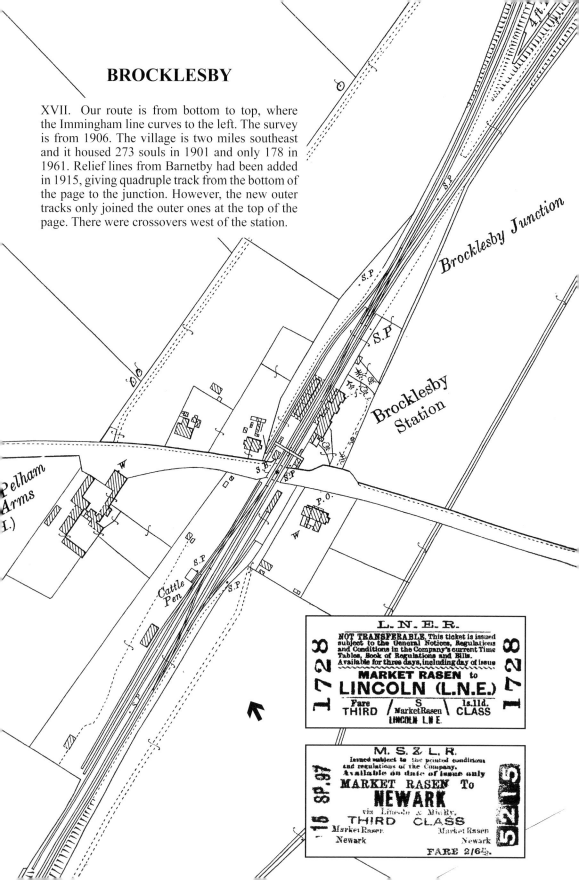

BROCKLESBY

XVII. Our route is from bottom to top, where the Immingham line curves to the left. The survey is from 1906. The village is two miles southeast and it housed 273 souls in 1901 and only 178 in 1961. Relief lines from Barnetby had been added in 1915, giving quadruple track from the bottom of the page to the junction. However, the new outer tracks only joined the outer ones at the top of the page. There were crossovers west of the station.

Brocklesby Junction

Brocklesby Station

Pelham Arms (L.)

Cattle Pen

57. The palatial styling is worth more than a glimpse, as everything from the ridge tiles to the door arches have commendable details. The up relief line was later a major intrusion, running along the foreground of this view.
(P.Laming coll.)

58. "Chips with everything" was once a much used phrase, but never "Fish with everything". Fish trains from Grimsby were common practice until the 1950s, but most stopped on the rails. This failure was on 27th March 1907, when a coal train was involved with the collision. Baldwin class 15 2-6-0 no. 966 had to be cut up on the site.
(P.Laming coll.)

59.   A view southwest from about 1939 has one of the goods sidings beyond the left half of the bridge. Its closure came on 3rd February 1964. The bridge had replaced a level crossing in about 1914. (Stations UK)

60   No. 47401 speeds into the station on 27th July 1979 with a Cleethorpes to Kings Cross express. Another class 47 waits with oil tankers from Immingham on the left. (T.Heavyside)

61.   The station was unstaffed from 29th June 1969 and is seen on 30th April 1986, as no. 47207 runs east with a Merry-Go-Round coal train. The 1914 box had 96 levers until replaced by a panel in 1998. Known as Brocklesby Junction, it was still in use in 2014. (J.Whitehouse)

62.   Nos 31199 and 31154 come off the Ulceby line on 24th November 1989, with a long train of petrol tankers, representing a regular freight flow from Immingham Port. The wide angled view shows the ornate station building to good effect. It was built for the second Earl of Yarborough, chairman of the MS&LR and local landowner. By 1989 it had long outlived its purpose. At this date the station lacked even the basic facility of a public telephone, but lingered on until closure from 3rd October 1993. The station building and the signalbox were given Grade II listed status under the care of English Heritage. (A.C.Hartless)

63.   The earlier four tracks between Brocklesby and Barnetby were reduced to two in the late 1980s, but one of the decommissioned tracks, the down (westbound) slow line, was reinstated in 1995 to cope with rising freight volumes. No. 37134 takes the Ulceby curve as it approaches Brocklesby with a barrier waggon and empty tanks on 30th April 1986. (J.Whitehouse)

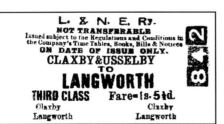

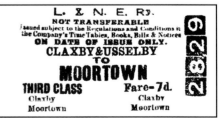

HABROUGH

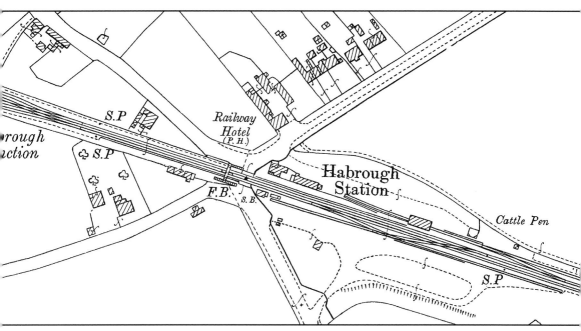

XVIII. The 1906 edition indicates that most of the village is north of the line. Its population was 344 in 1901, almost doubling by 1961.

64.   Our survey starts from the footbridge in about 1930 and this view east reveals that freight was handled on both sides of the line. The weigh bridge for road vehicles is on the right. (Stations UK)

65.   Activity was recorded at about the same time, as a down train approached. The hut on the left was the lamp room, which was always remote from other buildings, due to fire risk. (Stations UK)

66.   We now have a pair of photographs from 27th July 1979, this one featuring a DMU working from New Holland to Cleethorpes. It has used the line on the right from Habrough Junction. (T.Heavyside)

67. No. 55006 is passing through with a Cleethorpes to Kings Cross service. The gates were controlled by a wheel in the box, which had 28 levers. It was in use from 1883 until 18th September 1988. The station was unstaffed from June 1969 until October 1970. (T.Heavyside)

M. S. & L. R.
Issued subject to the printed conditions
and regulations of the Company
Available on date of issue only.

HOLTON
TO
BARNETBY
THIRD CLASS
FARE 9d.

8125

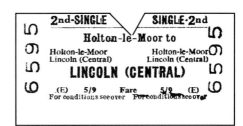

2nd-SINGLE   SINGLE-2nd
Holton-le-Moor to

Holton-le-Moor   Holton-le-Moor
Lincoln (Central)   Lincoln (Central)
LINCOLN (CENTRAL)

(E)   5/9   Fare   5/9   (E)
For conditions see over   For conditions see over

6595

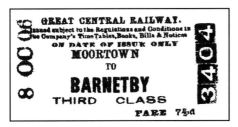

GREAT CENTRAL RAILWAY.
Issued subject to the Regulations and Conditions in
the Company's TimeTables, Books, Bills & Notices
ON DATE OF ISSUE ONLY
MOORTOWN
TO
BARNETBY
THIRD CLASS
FARE 7½d.

8 00 05   3404

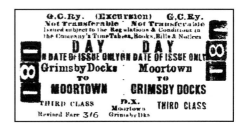

G.C.Ry. (Excursion)   G.C.Ry.
Not Transferable   Not Transferable
Issued subject to the Regulations & Conditions in
the Company's TimeTables, Books, Bills & Notices
DAY   DAY
ON DATE OF ISSUE ONLY ON DATE OF ISSUE ONLY
Grimsby Docks   Moortown
TO   TO
MOORTOWN   GRIMSBY DOCKS
THIRD CLASS   n.x.   THIRD CLASS
Moortown
Revised Fare 3/6   Grimsby Dks

181   181

68.   No. 150135 was working a Cleethorpes to Newark service on 23rd November 1989. This is a typical straight track in flat countryside. The platforms continue to be staggered and both will take four cars. (F.T.Hornby)

69.   The conductor of the 14.28 Cleethorpes to Manchester Airport is awaiting departure time on 30th November 2006. The unit is no. 185105 and is showing the First logo. It had just run by Roxton Sidings signal box of 1883. Its 18-lever frame was still in use in 2014. The sidings had earlier served a quarry. (A.C.Hartless)

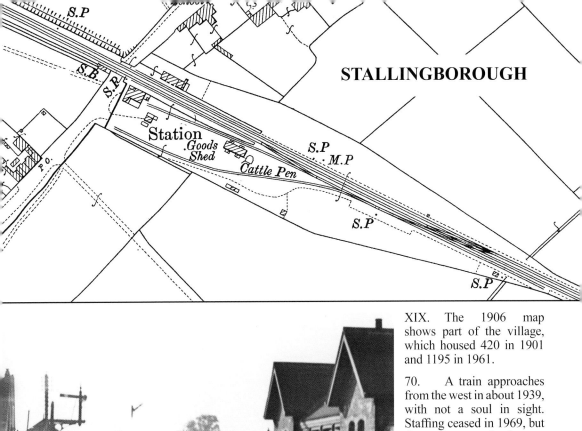

STALLINGBOROUGH

XIX. The 1906 map shows part of the village, which housed 420 in 1901 and 1195 in 1961.

70. A train approaches from the west in about 1939, with not a soul in sight. Staffing ceased in 1969, but the station remained open, as did the others to Grimsby. (Stations UK)

71. The goods yard closed on 25th May 1964, but the goods shed was still standing as seen shortly after track lifting. It contained a 30cwt crane. (Lens of Sutton coll.)

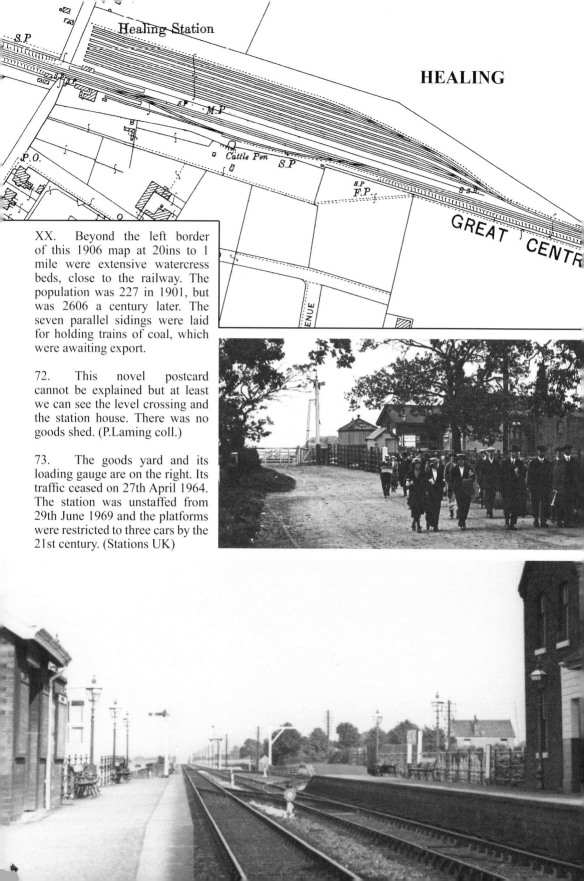

HEALING

Healing Station

S.P · M.P · Cattle Pen · S.P · P.O. · S.P F.P. · GREAT CENTR · ENUE

XX.   Beyond the left border of this 1906 map at 20ins to 1 mile were extensive watercress beds, close to the railway. The population was 227 in 1901, but was 2606 a century later. The seven parallel sidings were laid for holding trains of coal, which were awaiting export.

72.   This novel postcard cannot be explained but at least we can see the level crossing and the station house. There was no goods shed. (P.Laming coll.)

73.   The goods yard and its loading gauge are on the right. Its traffic ceased on 27th April 1964. The station was unstaffed from 29th June 1969 and the platforms were restricted to three cars by the 21st century. (Stations UK)

GREAT COATES

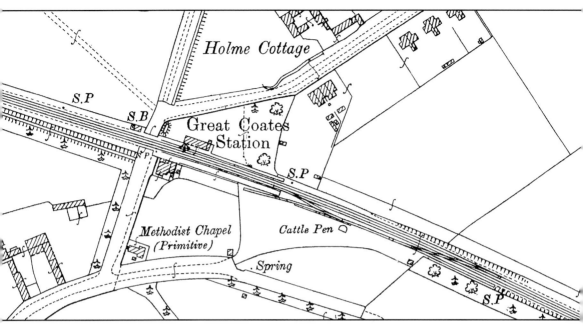

XXI.   The 1906 issue has some of the village nearby. Its population grew from 245 in 1841 to 364 in 1911. Boundary reduction resulted in a figure of 1111 in 2001.

74.   An up express speeds through in about 1939. White platform edges would soon be introduced, due to the black out of World War II; lime wash was used. (Stations UK)

75.   Sadly undated, this fine record features no. 62666 *Zeebrugge*. This was one of the class D11 4-4-0s introduced in 1920 and known as "Large Directors". A least five young spotters are present. The signal box was completed in 1884 and had a 39-lever frame. It was in use until 18th October 1987, by which time the up platform was authorised for use by three cars and the down one by four. (R.B.Parr/SLS coll.)

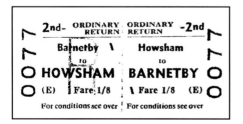

76.　　The down side and its approach steps are seen in about 1960. The station was unstaffed from 25th May 1964, but it was later to serve a large suburban development of Grimsby. (Lens of Sutton coll.)

77.　　No. 185134 speeds through on 30th November 2006, forming the 09.52 Manchester Airport to Cleethorpes. There were identical shelters on both platforms by that time. The next signal box to pass would be Marsh Junction. This was of GCR design and opened in 1907. It was fitted with a 44-lever frame and was still open in 2014. (A.C.Hartless)

WEST OF GRIMSBY TOWN

XXII.   The Railway Clearing House route map is from 1911 and we arrive on the line marked "From Sheffield" at Marsh Junction. The left route north to the docks and the left curve date from 1879, the right curve being added in 1906. The tracks from Immingham into the docks opened in 1910. The electric line is not shown, as it came in 1912. It terminated at Corporation Bridge and ran until 1961, although the eastern extremity closed in 1956. The 1907 Marsh Junction Box had 44 levers and was still in use in 2014. Alexandra Dock (south end) had started as The Haven in 1799 and the western part came in 1880. The Royal Dock dated from 1852, Fish Dock No. 1 from 1856, No. 2 from 1877 and No. 3 from 1934. It was created in the bay east of No. 2.

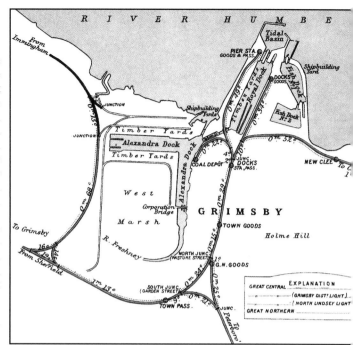

78.   Co-acting home and distant semaphores dominate the scene at Friargate Crossing as class 114 cars E53018 and E54033 pass with the 11.15 from Newark North Gate to Cleethorpes on 11th April 1984. Friargate Crossing box was a good example of the MS&LR's second design of box, introduced in 1880. It was destroyed by fire in June 1990. It had 14 levers. In the background is Littlefield Crossing Box, which had 13 levers and functioned from 1884 until 26th September 1993. (P.D.Shannon)

GRIMSBY TOWN

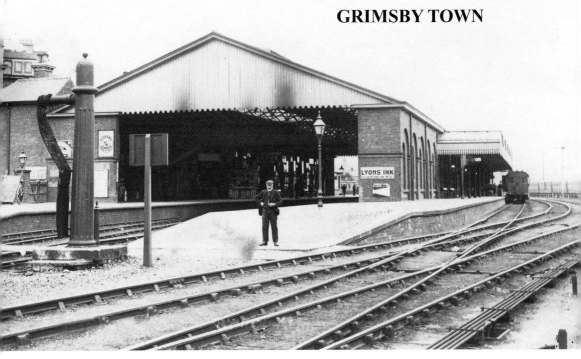

79.   Postmarked 1906, this card shows the west end of the station at about the time of the survey. The suffix TOWN had been added in 1900. (P.Laming coll.)

80.   Another postcard and this is from about 1909, showing the north elevation. The cattle dock was immediately west of the station, adjacent to the cattle market. The canopy and its massive stanchions were still in place into the 21st century. (Lens of Sutton coll.)

XXIII. On the right is the town's third gasworks. It opened in November 1877 and it consumed 9869 tons of coal in 1909. It used about 65,000 tons in 1951 and closed in about 1961. The 1907 edition has our route from the left to the top, with the former ELR from the south lower right. Spend time on this to enjoy it to the full. The curve between the two was in use from 1848 to 1980, when the line from the south from Louth closed for freight. Passenger service had ceased in 1970.

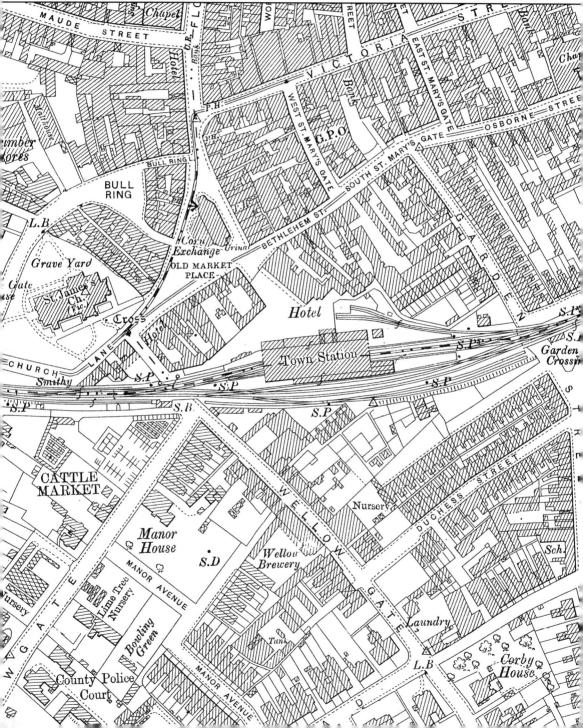

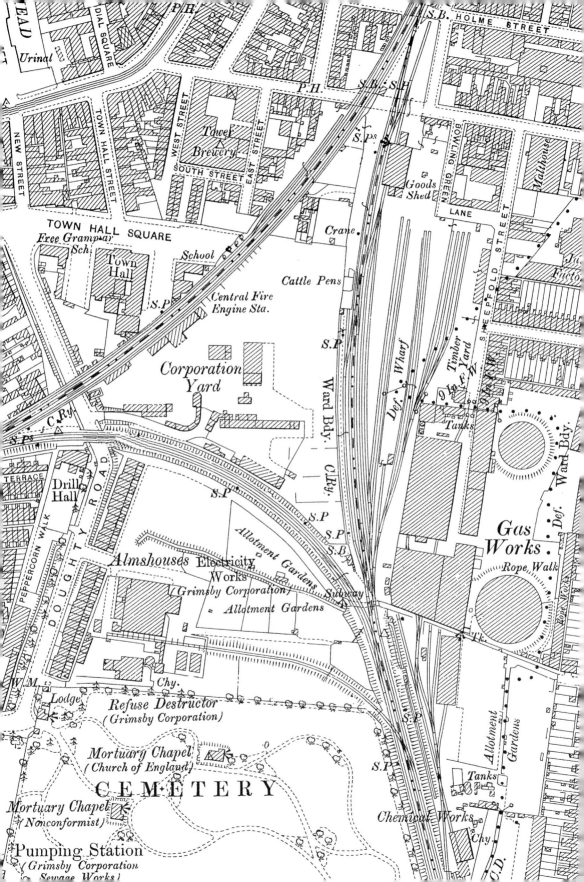

81.   Now we see the east end in April 1947. There were about 300 trawlers still active at that time. Grim was a Danish fisherman who started trading here about 1000 years earlier, when the community grew to around 200. (H.C.Casserley)

82.   The west end was recorded on 16th April 1947 as class K3 2-6-0 no. 1834 waits to leave with the 2.51pm to Peterborough. The businesses for which there were private sidings included creosote, bitumen, timber, shipbuilding, gasworks, tanning, coal, cod liver oil, electricity, highways, nightsoil, ice, wagon repairs and saw mills. (H.C.Casserley)

83.	A 1961 picture has one of the large hotels to the left of the water tank and two freight docks in line with it. On the left is platform 3, outside the main roof. The population was 8860 in 1851, 96,350 in 1961 and 159,600 in 2011. (Stations UK)

84.	A new roof had arrived over platforms 1 and 2 by the time that no. 55021 was recorded on 28th July 1979, but the old footbridge was retained under it. Mailbag barrows are evident, but that traffic would soon end. The 1962 "Deltic" class locomotive carried the name *Argyll and Sutherland Highlander* from 1973 until its withdrawal in 1981. (T.Heavyside)

85.   Two class 114 units await their next duty at Grimsby Town on 5th June 1980. At that time all trains serving Grimsby ran through to/from Cleethorpes, except on Winter Sundays, when Grimsby Town acted as terminus. (P.D.Shannon)

86.   Cravens class 105 cars E51284 and E56446 pass Wellowgate box forming the 09.25 Doncaster to Cleethorpes train on 12th April 1983. Wellowgate box was a MS&LR type 2 design, dating back to the 1880s. It closed on 29th September 1993 when control of the level crossing passed to Pasture Street box. The former was saved by the National Railway Museum. (P.D.Shannon)

87.   The new roof appears to have been designed for the steam era, but at least the echoes were reduced. The panels were complete above the footbridge for comfort. No. 156468 was photographed on 10th May 1999. (M.Turvey)

88.   This panorama is from Wellowgate footbridge on 30th November 2006 and no. 153365 has just arrived at platform 3 from Newark North Gate. This had a new roof covering, but the old brickwork was retained. All the platforms were listed for seven cars. (A.C.Hartless)

EAST OF GRIMSBY TOWN

89.   Garden Street Junction Box was at the end of the platforms, which can be seen in the next picture. No. 8069 is one of a batch of 75 0-6-0STs bought from the Ministry of Supply after the war, in 1946. The locomotive is approaching platform 2. (H.C.Casserley)

90.   Class 105 no. 54440 is departing for Cleethorpes on 30th April 1986. The 1881 signal box had 39 levers and was worked until 26th September 1993. Being a listed structure it was boarded up and remained so 20 years later. (J.Whitehouse)

SOUTH OF GRIMSBY DOCKS

91.   Pasture Street signal box was at the northern apex of the triangular junction (see diagram near picture 78). Passing it on 30th November 2006 is no. 185105 and it is running away from us, bound for Cleethorpes. It is about to pass onto the single track section to a loop created south of Docks station. On the right is the end of the line from platform 3, extended to the top of the last map. This shows three running lines and a siding on the west side of the triangle. (A.C.Hartless)

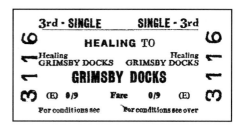

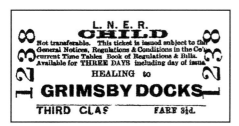

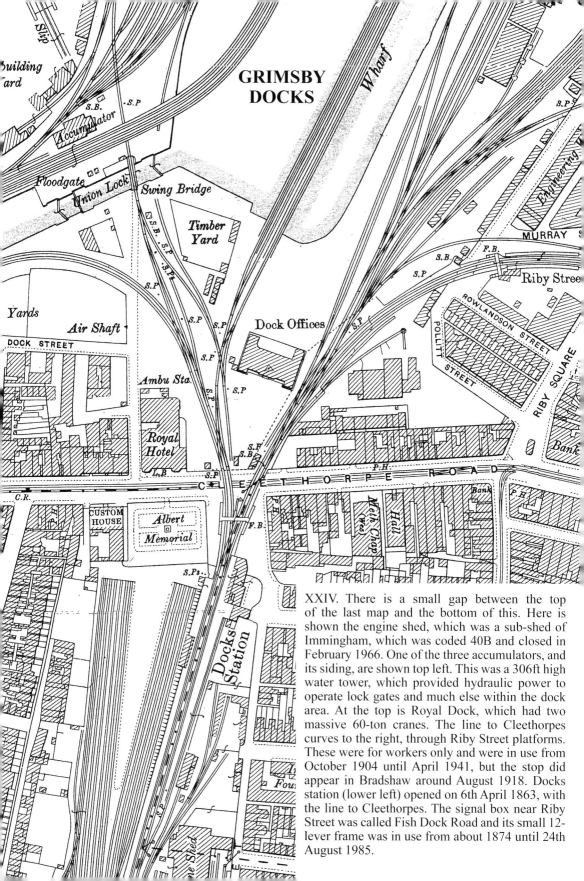

GRIMSBY DOCKS

XXIV. There is a small gap between the top of the last map and the bottom of this. Here is shown the engine shed, which was a sub-shed of Immingham, which was coded 40B and closed in February 1966. One of the three accumulators, and its siding, are shown top left. This was a 306ft high water tower, which provided hydraulic power to operate lock gates and much else within the dock area. At the top is Royal Dock, which had two massive 60-ton cranes. The line to Cleethorpes curves to the right, through Riby Street platforms. These were for workers only and were in use from October 1904 until April 1941, but the stop did appear in Bradshaw around August 1918. Docks station (lower left) opened on 6th April 1863, with the line to Cleethorpes. The signal box near Riby Street was called Fish Dock Road and its small 12-lever frame was in use from about 1874 until 24th August 1985.

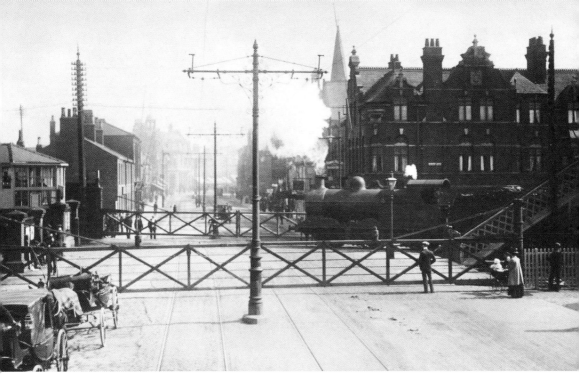

92.   This is the view east along Cleethorpes Road, which is shown across the middle of the map. Clearer on it are the four railway tracks and those of the tramway. Electric trams ran to Cleethorpes from 1901 to 1937; horse-drawn ones started in Grimsby in 1881, but were local. (P.Laming coll.)

93.   A postcard panorama from around 1900 features interesting crowd control arrangements and a splendid signal gantry. (P.Laming coll.)

94.　　We are on the footbridge looking south in about 1939, with the junction points in the foreground. Chimneys devoid of pots were an unusual feature. (Stations UK)

95.　　No. 8976 was a class J50/3, 0-6-0T, a type introduced in 1926. It is running south on dock lines on 10th May 1946. (H.C.Casserley)

96. Looking north on 19th April 1947, the main building is that of Grimsby Dock Offices. The lattice structure is a footbridge, with four flights of steps. (H.C.Casserley)

97. No. 31432 departs with the 12.45 Cleethorpes to Manchester Piccadilly on 30th April 1986. The level crossing seen in picture 92 caused immense road congestion. The replacement flyover from 1967 can be seen level with the first floor office windows. (J.Whitehouse)

98.   A closer view of the platforms on the same day reveals that the down one had no track by that time; the route had been singled to Cleethorpes. Derby-built class 114 no. 53035 was working a local service from Cleethorpes to Barton-on-Humber. (J.Whitehouse)

99.   The bridge carrying the A180 is clearer without the footbridge. The basic shelter and new rails were recorded on 30th November 2006. The platform was then suitable for only four coaches. (A.C.Hartless)

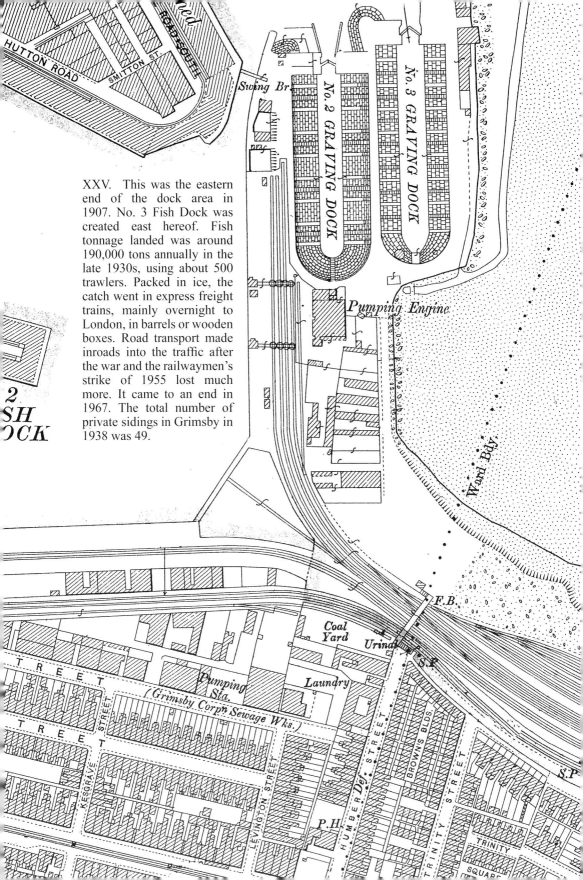

HUTTON ROAD

SMITTON ST

Swing Br.

No. 2 GRAVING DOCK

No. 3 GRAVING DOCK

Pumping Engine

Ward Bdy.

2
SH
OCK

XXV. This was the eastern end of the dock area in 1907. No. 3 Fish Dock was created east hereof. Fish tonnage landed was around 190,000 tons annually in the late 1930s, using about 500 trawlers. Packed in ice, the catch went in express freight trains, mainly overnight to London, in barrels or wooden boxes. Road transport made inroads into the traffic after the war and the railwaymen's strike of 1955 lost much more. It came to an end in 1967. The total number of private sidings in Grimsby in 1938 was 49.

F.B.

Coal
Yard

Urinal

S.P.

T R E E T

S T R E E T

Laundry

Pumping
Sta.
(Grimsby Corpⁿ Sewage Wks.)

KESGRAVE STREET

LEVINGTON STREET

Humber Def. STREET

BROWNS BLDS.

TRINITY STREET

S.P.

P.H.

TRINITY

TRINITY SQUARE

NEW CLEE

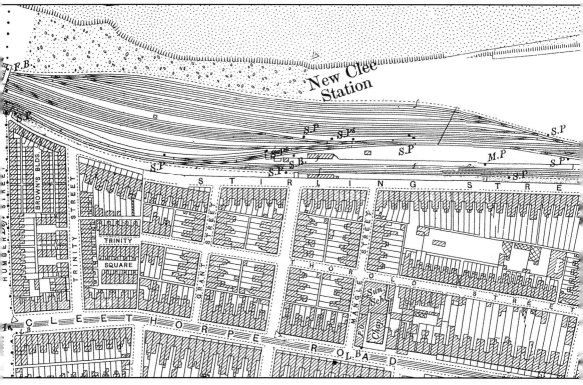

XXVI. The 1907 edition is shown at 20ins to 1 mile and overlaps the previous extract. The insert top right is the eastward continuation.

100.   This eastward panorama is from about 1939 and features the seaward facing dwellings of Stirling Street. The station was late on the scene, not opening until 1st July 1875. (Stations UK)

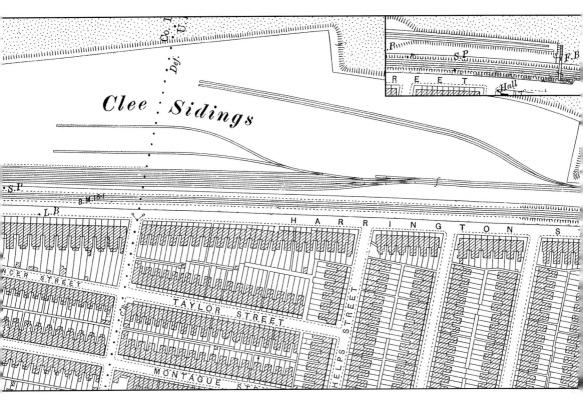

101.   A view in the other direction includes the road bridge built to serve the 1934 No. 3 Fish Dock. This was the second signal box on the site and it opened in about 1932. It had 46 levers and closed on 31st May 1970. After the singling, only the up platform remained, but it could take seven coaches. (Lens of Sutton coll.)

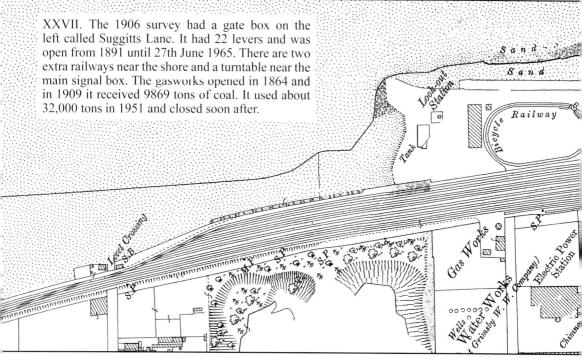

XXVII. The 1906 survey had a gate box on the left called Suggitts Lane. It had 22 levers and was open from 1891 until 27th June 1965. There are two extra railways near the shore and a turntable near the main signal box. The gasworks opened in 1864 and in 1909 it received 9869 tons of coal. It used about 32,000 tons in 1951 and closed soon after.

102. The arrival of an excursion was an impressive subject for a late Victorian postcard. All six platforms can be seen, along with the main building on the left and the promenade on the right. (Lens of Sutton coll.)

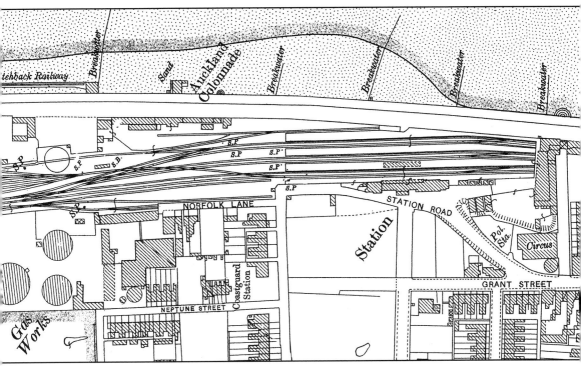

103.   This is the exit that the crowds were seeking and many of the tall buildings would provide the necessary accommodation for those on more than a day trip. (P.Laming coll.)

104.   A fine panorama emphasises the convenience of the station to the pleasure areas. At 300ft, the pier was almost as long as Grimsby's tallest accumulator. Station Road curves on the right. (P.Laming coll.)

105.   A closer view from the Edwardian era reveals that no flesh could be displayed, not even an ankle. There was a gate in the fence in the distance, near a small wharf where the horses and carriages of the wealthy could be unloaded from trains. (P.Laming coll.)

106.   This part of our survey was recorded from platform 1 in about 1912. The arches on the left are over the windows of the spacious refreshment room. There were goods sidings behind the camera until 7th December 1964 and there was a 5-ton crane, in later years. (Stations UK)

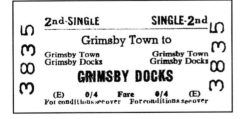

107.   Here are the gates and loading dock mentioned in caption 105. Class C4 4-4-2 stands with the 9.40am to New Holland on 9th May 1946. Engine cleaning was low priority in the austerity years of the post-war era. (H.C.Casserley)

108.   It is 1961 and more prosperous times brought a new canopy over the concourse. The platforms were not renumbered, although the centre four were then the ones used by most passengers. (Stations UK)

109.   Seen in 1961, the end of the station remained little altered, much of the fine tracery still remaining. The population was 12,578 in 1901, this rising to 33,220 by 1961. (R.M.Casserley)

110.   No. E56044 formed the 17.31 to Sheffield on 28th July 1979 and stands at platform 3. No. 4 lost its track later and No. 5 became No. 4. (T.Heavyside)

111.   In the background is the 100-lever signal box, which functioned from about 1889 until 28th April 1985. Hybrid class 123/124 DMU leaves for Manchester on 28th May 1981. Siemens later established its Traincare Facility on the right. (D.H.Mitchell)

112.   Locomotive haulage returned to some Lincolnshire services in the mid-1980s before the introduction of second generation diesel units. No. 31436 arrives with the 12.07 from Newark North Gate on 11th April 1984. On the left is a gas oil tank for the railway fuelling point; it would have been brought here from Lindsey Refinery, just a few miles away. (P.D.Shannon)

113.   Nos E54043 and E54044 stand at platform 1 on 25th July 1987, waiting to depart to Barton-on-Humber. The engine release crossover was retained here and part of it can be seen in the foreground. (D.H.Mitchell)

114.   Two views from 23rd June 1999 record the original buildings. This is the road side and some new uses had been found, including rooms for train crew. (A.C.Hartless)

115.   All four platforms could accommodate eight cars; nos 1 and 3 are occupied here. A good and diverse service continued to be provided. (A.C.Hartless)

CLEETHORPES COAST LIGHT RAILWAY

Cleethorpes Kingsway
116.   Pictured on 10th May 1999 is the Ravenglass & Eskdale Railway's no. 6, a vertical-boilered 0-4-0 from 1995, named *Flower of the Forest*. (M.Turvey)

XXVIII. The line was laid at 10¼ ins gauge in 1948 and was converted to 14½ ins in 1972. The final change was made in 1994, when 15ins track was introduced. The section from Lakeside to Humberside North Sea Lane was opened for the 2007 season. By 2013, four steam locomotives were operating, plus three diesels and 13 coaches. There was much additional stock from

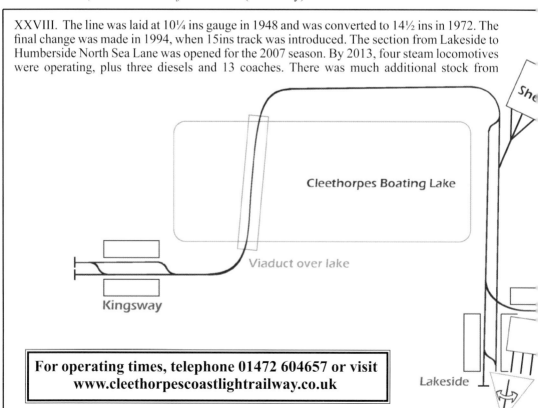

For operating times, telephone 01472 604657 or visit
www.cleethorpescoastlightrailway.co.uk

other collections. This is the 2014 track diagram. The "Lollipop Express" road train has operated between the Pier and Kingsway for much of the Summer, in many years. (A.Cowood)

117. This and the following photographs were taken on 9th July 2011 and most include no. 1 *Sutton Belle*, a 4-4-2 built by Cannon Iron Foundries in 1933. (P.G.Barnes)

North Sea Lane

Meridian Park
Events Arena

Theme Park

Cleethorpes Lakeside

118.   Few crossing lights are taller than their trains; these were installed in 2000, near the station. There were two sets of flood gates across the track nearby. (P.G.Barnes)

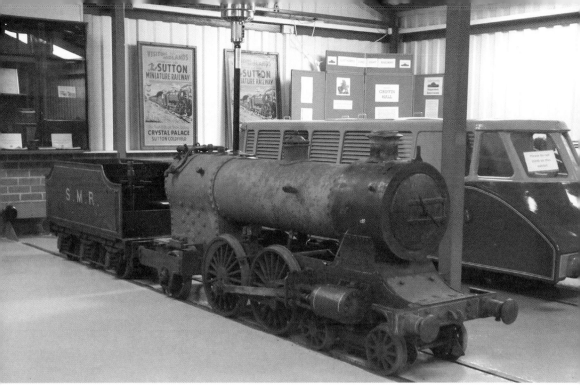

119.   The Seaside Miniature Railway Museum was opened in the Griffon Hall at the station in 2005. Nearest is the *Mighty Atom*, which was built by Bassett-Lowke in 1909 and later renamed *Prince of Wales*. Behind it is No. 4, a Bo-Bo diesel from G&S Light Engineering in 1946. (P.G.Barnes)

Humberside North Sea Lane

120.   The extension to this station was 900 yards long. The terminus was built on the site of one used by the Lincolnshire Coast Light Railway from the 1960s to 1980. (P.G.Barnes)